dogs

A PHOTOGRAPHIC CELEBRATION

Metro Books
122 Fifth Avenue
New York, NY 10011

ISBN-13: 978-0-7607-9026-7
ISBN-10: 0-7607-9026-4

Printed and bound in China

3 5 7 9 10 8 6 4 2

dogs

A PHOTOGRAPHIC CELEBRATION

edited by rachael Ianicci and
franchesca ho sang

METRO BOOKS
NEW YORK

"Dogs are miracles with paws."
—SUSAN ARIEL RAINBOW KENNEDY

The beagle is one of the only dog breeds that do not drool.

"To err is human, to forgive, canine."
—ANONYMOUS

Unlike most dog breeds, Chihuahuas are frequently finicky eaters.

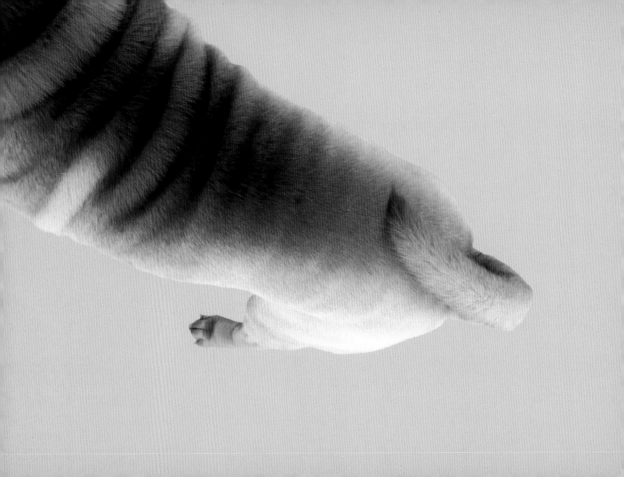

"Dogs laugh, but they laugh with their tails."
—MAX EASTMAN

Dogs shed naturally in the spring and fall, but due to artificial light, indoor dogs may shed all year long.

"Every dog must have his day."
—Jonathan Swift

When a dog pants, its tongue can swell to two or three times
its normal size, which helps release body heat.

"Whoever said you can't buy happiness forgot little puppies."
—GENE HILL

Golf courses use border collies to chase geese away.

"We long for an affection altogether ignorant of our faults.
Heaven has accorded this to us in the
uncritical canine attachment."
—GEORGE ELIOT

The American Staffordshire terrier can be traced back to the original bulldogs in England, which were used in the bloody sport of bull baiting.

"Children and dogs are as necessary to the
welfare of the country as Wall Street and the railroads."
—Harry S Truman

A puppy has 28 milk teeth.

"Scratch a dog and you will find a permanent job."
—Franklin P. Jones

The name *shar-pei* means "sand-skin," which refers to the unique quality of the shar-pei's sandpaperlike coat.

"Let sleeping dogs lie."
—CHARLES DICKENS

Dogs have been domesticated for at least 100,000 years.

The wrinkles on a bulldog's face channel blood away
from its nostrils when it locks its jaws on a bull's nose.

The yarn chiengora is made of dog hair.

"A dog is the only thing on earth that loves you more than he loves himself."
—JOSH BILLINGS

The boxer was one of the first breeds selected in Germany for police training.

"I love a dog. He does nothing for political reasons."
—WILL ROGERS

Puppies are born blind and deaf.

"A good dog deserves a good bone."
—Ben Johnson

Toto from *The Wizard of Oz* was a Cairn terrier.

"A dog has the soul of a philosopher."
—PLATO

The name *basset* comes from the French adjective *bas*, which means "low thing" or "dwarf."

"The best thing about a man is his dog."
—ANONYMOUS

Dalmatian puppies are born without spots.

"A barking dog is often more useful than a sleeping lion."
—WASHINGTON IRVING

One in every four dogs is overweight.

"I would rather see the portrait of a dog that I know, than all the allegorical paintings they can show me in the world."

—SAMUEL JOHNSON

The average dog has about 100 different facial expressions,
but bulldogs and pit bulls are capable of making only 10.
These 10 expressions are easily misinterpreted by other dogs,
which may explain why bulldogs and pit bulls often get into fights.

"My little dog—a heartbeat at my feet."
—EDITH WHARTON

Aggression in dogs is one of the most common
problems that prompt dog owners to seek professional assistance.

"There are three faithful friends: an old wife, an old dog, and ready money."
—BENJAMIN FRANKLIN

A dog yawns as a sign of contentment.

"Money will buy a pretty good dog, but it won't buy the wag of his tail."
—Josh Billings

The Australian cattle dog was once called the Australian heeler,
and it is still sometimes called the blue or Queensland heeler today.

"A man's soul can be judged by the way he treats his dog."
—Charles Doran

The chow chow originated in Mongolia and northern China, where it is called *songshi quan*, which translates to "puffy lion dog."

"Dogs are our link to paradise. They don't know evil or jealousy or discontent."
—Milan Kundera

One way dogs release body heat is by panting.

"The pug is living proof that God has a sense of humor."
—Margot Kaufman

The expression "three dog night" allegedly refers to extremely cold nights
when Australian aborigines would sleep with
three dogs to keep from freezing.

"If a dog's prayers were answered,
bones would rain from the sky."
—Proverb

Dogs see in color.

"Be on your guard against a silent dog and still water."
—LATIN PROVERB

The Doberman pinscher was first bred in Germany by Ludwig Dobermann, a tax collector who needed a guard dog for protection.

"If a dog jumps in your lap, it is because he is fond of you."
—ALFRED NORTH WHITEHEAD

The national dog of Cuba is the Havanese.

"The most affectionate creature in the world is a wet dog."
—AMBROSE BIERCE

A dog sweats through its nose and footpads.

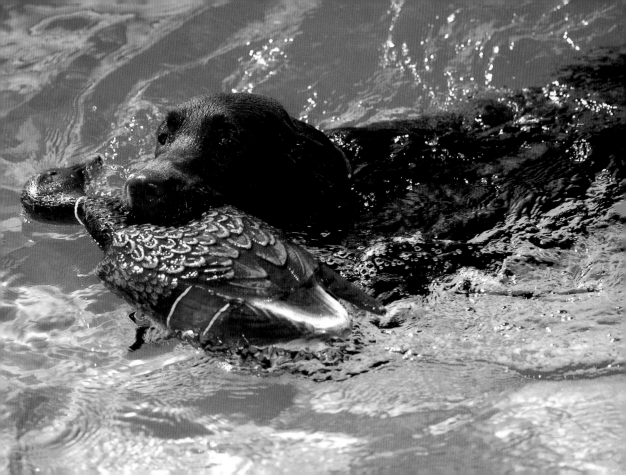

"A man's best friend is his dog."
—Lord Byron

Light-colored dogs can get sunburned.

"The average dog has one request to all humankind. Love me."
—HELEN EXLEY

The pug is a common pet in Buddhist monasteries.

"I would look at a dog and when our eyes met, I realized that the dog and all creatures are my family. They're like you and me."
—ZIGGY MARLEY

"Mixed breeds" and "crossbreeds" are not the same.
Mixed breed dogs have multiple lineages that are usually unknown.
Crossbreeds are the product of only two different breeds of dogs.

"Never stand between a dog and the hydrant."
—John Peers

The highest number of surviving puppies from a single birth is 20.

"We never really own a dog as much as he owns us."
—GENE HILL

The first seeing-eye dog was presented to a blind person on April 25, 1938.

"Necessity has the face of a dog."
—GABRIEL GARCÍA MÁRQUEZ

The greyhound is the second-fastest land animal
and the fastest dog breed, topping out at speeds of 45 miles per hour.

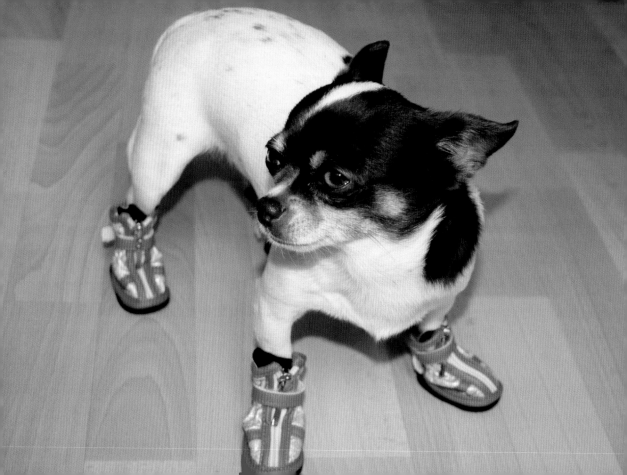

"If friends fail us, if the phone is silent and the postman passes
Our dog will touch our knee, and smile, and say
Who cares? All the more time for us to be together
Come for a walk. This is a splendid day."
—Pam Brown

Eating grass may help to ease the upset stomach of a dog.

"A dog teaches a boy fidelity, perseverance,
and to turn around three times before lying down."
—ROBERT BENCHLEY

One of the oldest breeds of dog is the saluki.

"When most of us talk to our dogs, we tend to forget they are not people."
—Julia Glass

A dog's sense of smell is so keen that if a pot of soup were cooking, the dog could discern all of the individual ingredients.

French bulldogs are easily identified by their bat ears
and half-flat, half-domed skull.

"It is fatal to let any dog know that he is funny,
for he immediately loses his head and starts hamming it up."
—P. G. WODEHOUSE

Among the very few who survived the sinking of the *Titanic* were two dogs that made it to safety on one of the first lifeboats.

"Living with a dog is easy—like living with an idealist."
—H. L. MENCKEN

The bulldog serves as mascot for England, the U.S. Marines, and Yale University.

"A dog knows the places he is thrown food."
—African proverb

Chocolate can be fatal to dogs.

"If you think dogs can't count, try putting three dog biscuits in your pocket and then giving Fido only two of them."
—PHIL PASTORET

The name *papillion* means "butterfly" in French.

"The dog is a gentleman; I hope to go to his heaven, not man's."
—MARK TWAIN

Basset hounds have the longest ears in proportion
to their heads and body size of any of the dog breeds.

"To a dog the whole world is a smell."
—ANONYMOUS

In the movie *One Hundred and One Dalmatians,*
Pongo has 72 spots, Perdita has 68, and each of the puppies has 32.

"The biggest dog has been a pup."
—Joaquin Miller

The Newfoundland is still used in Newfoundland
and Labrador to pull carts and carry packages.

"Don't accept your dog's admiration as conclusive evidence that you are wonderful."
—Ann Landers

Traditionally, Doberman pinschers have had both tail and ears cropped.
In some countries, docking and cropping are now illegal.

"Things that upset a Terrier may pass virtually unnoticed by a Great Dane."
—SMILEY BLANTON

The most popular names for male dogs are
Max, Buddy, Jake, Rocky, Bailey, Buster, Charlie,
Sam, Lucky, Cody, Toby, Jack, Shadow, Duke, and Rusty.

"One reason a dog can be such a comfort when you're feeling blue
is that he doesn't try to find out why."
—ANONYMOUS

Don't blow into a dog's ear; this can cause injury.

"The poor dog, in life the firmest friend,
The first to welcome, foremost to defend,
Whose honest heart is still the master's own,
Who labors, fights, lives, breathes for him alone,
Unhonour'd falls, unnoticed all his worth,
Denied in heaven the soul he held on earth,
While man, vain insect hopes to be forgiven,
And claims himself a sole exclusive heaven."
—LORD BYRON

The Alaskan malamute is one of the oldest arctic sled dogs.

"All knowledge, the totality of all questions and all answers, is contained in the dog."
—Franz Kafka

The ancestors of the Akita were once used as hunting dogs in Japan.

"I am I because my little dog knows me."
—GERTRUDE STEIN

Dogs, like humans, are either left-handed or right-handed.

"The greatest love is a mother's; then a dog's; then a sweetheart's."
—POLISH PROVERB

You can tell how a dog feels by observing the way it stands.
How it holds its head, ears, eyes, and tail are also telltale signs of its mood.

"Acquiring a dog may be the only opportunity
a human ever has to choose a relative."
—MORDECAI SIEGAL

Never disturb a dog while it is eating. This may scare it and cause it to attack.

"Every dog is a lion at home."
—H. G. BOHN

When Pompeii was destroyed by Mount Vesuvius in 79 CE, searchers found evidence of a dog lying across a child, apparently trying to save it.

"A bone to the dog is not charity. Charity is the bone shared with the dog, when you are just as hungry as the dog."
—JACK LONDON

It was once common practice to carry a
Maltese in the folds of clothing or in a sleeve.

"If you want loyalty—get a dog. If you want loyalty and attention—get a smart dog."
—GRANT FAIRLEY

The Dalai Lama once presented powerful
emperors with Lhasa apsos dogs as good luck symbols.

"A dog doesn't care if you're rich or poor, big or small, young or old.
He doesn't care if you're not smart, not popular, not a good joke-teller,
not the best athlete, nor the best-looking person. To your dog, you are the greatest,
the smartest, the nicest human being who was ever born.
You are his friend and protector."
—LOUIS SABIN

The basenji is the only dog that does not bark.

"Some days you're the dog. Some days you're the hydrant."
—Anonymous

Beagles are one of the most popular breeds among U.S. presidents. Lyndon B. Johnson owned three, named "Him," "Her," and "Edgar."

Spaying and neutering a pet not only protects it against certain cancers and infections, but also helps to control the animal population.

Bloodhounds possess the keenest sense of smell of all dog breeds.
They are commonly used to track missing persons,
escaped prisoners, and disaster victims.

"From a dog's point of view, his master is an elongated and abnormally cunning dog."
—MABEL L. ROBINSON

Bull terriers rarely bark.

"The average dog is a nicer person than the average person."
—ANDREW A. ROONEY

The Cavalier King Charles spaniel was named after King Charles I of Britain.

"When a dog gets a bone, he doesn't go out
and make a down payment on a bigger bone.
He buries the one he's got."
—WILL ROGERS

Small terriers were once kept around stables and on farms to keep rats away.

"The dog has got more fun out of man than man has got out of the dog, for the clearly demonstrable reason that man is the more laughable of the two animals."
—James Thurber

The elegant Afghan hound is an ancient breed:
depictions of it have been found on cave walls in northern Afghanistan
that date back more than 4,000 years.

"A dog running for joy of living is happiness personified."
—PETER GRAY

The American Eskimo dog, or Eskie, was once a popular trick dog, traveling with many circuses in the nineteenth century.

"The dog lives for the day, the hour, even the moment."
—ROBERT FALCON SCOTT

During World War I, Stubby, an American Staffordshire terrier, earned the rank of Sergeant.

"If they need a buddy, let them buy a dog."
—WHITEY HERZOG

The shar-pei is one of two breeds with a blue-black tongue.

"Our dog chases people on a bike. We've had to take it off him."
—Winston Churchill

For hundreds of years, the borzoi was bred by the Russian aristocracy.

An English mastiff holds the record of heaviest dog, weighing 343 pounds at the age of eight in 1989.

The term *bloodhound* refers not to the way a bloodhound trails, but to the efforts to maintain as pure a breed as possible.

"A dog wags its tail with its heart."
—MARTIN BUXBAUM

The American Staffordshire terrier is also known as the pit bull.

"You can say any foolish thing to a dog, and the dog will give you a look that says,
'My God, you're right! I never would've thought of that!'"
—Dave Barry

Chihuahuas prefer companions of their own breed.

"Many who have spent a lifetime in it can tell us less of love than the child that lost a dog yesterday."
—THORNTON WILDER

The designation "cocker spaniel" can refer to either the American cocker spaniel or the English cocker spaniel, which are two separate breeds.

"Happiness is a warm puppy."
—CHARLES SCHULZ

During World War I, Americans took to calling their dachshunds "liberty pups" to avoid any association with Germany.

"A dog is not 'almost human' and I know of no greater insult to the canine race than to describe it as such."
—JOHN HOLMES

The dalmatian is a dog of many names. It is also referred to as the English coach-dog, the carriage dog, the plum pudding dog, and the spotted Dick.

"Dogs' lives are too short. Their only fault, really."
—Agnes Sligh Turnbull

Certain types of common mushrooms, when ingested
or even licked by a dog, can prove fatal.

"The one absolutely unselfish friend that man
can have in this selfish world,
the one that never deserts him,
the one that never proves ungrateful
or treacherous, is his dog."
—George Graham Vest

You'll find a dog in approximately one in every three American households.

"Blessed is the person who has earned the love of an old dog."
—SYDNEY JEANNE SEWARD

The chow chow has a blue-black tongue.

Chihuahuas were named after the Mexican state of Chihuahua.

The Labrador retriever is the most popular dog breed
in the United States, Canada, and the United Kingdom.

"No man can be condemned for owning a dog. As long as he has a dog, he has a friend; and the poorer he gets, the better friend he has."
—WILL ROGERS

Löwchen means "little lion" in German.

"Dogs love company.
They place it first in their short list of needs."
—J. R. ACKERLEY

Tibetan mastiffs are called *do-khyi* ("tied dog") in Tibet, where they are kept chained to gates during the day and let loose at night.

"One reason a dog is such a lovable creature is his tail wags instead of his tongue."
—Anonymous

It is estimated that there are 6.5 million dogs in the United Kingdom.

When frightened, a dog pulls his tail between
his legs to cover the scent glands in his anal region.

The average dog has more than 200 million scent receptors.

"There is no psychiatrist in the world like a puppy licking your face."
—BEN WILLIAMS

Weimaraner puppies are striped at birth.

"Thorns may hurt you, men desert you, sunlight turn to fog;
but you're never friendless ever, if you have a dog."
—DOUGLAS MALLOCK

Standard schnauzers were used by the German army as Red Cross aides.

"When a man's best friend is his dog, that dog has a problem."
—Edward Abbey

Because of their large heads, bulldog puppies are usually delivered by cesarean section.

"Thou call'st me dog before thou hadst a cause, But since I am a dog, beware my fangs . . ."
—WILLIAM SHAKESPEARE

The boxer gets its name because it strikes out with its front paws when fighting.

"Whoever else thinks you are of little worth—
to your dog you are the center of the universe . . ."
—PAM BROWN

Shibas are considered the oldest of Japan's dogs.

"The bond with a true dog is as lasting as the ties of this earth will ever be."
—Konrad Lorenz

Dogs are omnivores.

"Heaven goes by favor. If it went by merit,
you would stay out and your dog would go in."
—MARK TWAIN

Never sneak up on a sleeping dog. If you startle it, it might bite you before it fully awakens.

"If a dog will not come to you after having looked you in the face, you should go home and examine your conscience."
—Woodrow Wilson

Pembroke Welsh corgis are born without tails.

"Once a dog loves you, he loves you always, no matter what you do, no matter what happens, no matter how much time goes by."
—JEFFREY MASSON

The Alaskan malamute was originally bred to pull sleds.

"He cannot be a gentleman which loveth not a dog."
—JOHN NORTHBROOKE

The papillion was once named the "dwarf spaniel."

"A reasonable amount of fleas is good for a dog;
it keeps him from brooding over being a dog."
—E. N. WESTCOTT

Dalmatians are famous for being firehouse dogs.

"Histories are more full of examples of the fidelity of dogs than of friends."
—ALEXANDER POPE

John Wayne owned an Airedale named Little Duke.

"What counts is not necessarily the size of the dog in the fight;
it's the size of the fight in the dog."
—DWIGHT D. EISENHOWER

While imprisoned at Les Carmes, Joséphine Bonaparte
sent secret messages to her husband, Napoleon,
by tucking them into the collar of her pet pug, Fortune.

The practice of licking an owner's face may stem from puppyhood, when a canine licks his mother's face for leftovers.

The dachshund was bred in Germany more than 300 years ago to hunt badgers.

"If you are a dog and your owner suggests
that you wear a sweater . . . suggest that he wear a tail."
—Fran Lebowitz

The most popular companion dog in Japan is the Shiba Inu.

"The great pleasure of a dog is that you make a fool of yourself with him and not only will he not scold you, but he will make a fool of himself too."
—SAMUEL BUTLER

Chow chows were once bred for food.

"The dog has seldom been successful in pulling man up to its level of sagacity, but man has frequently dragged the dog down to his."
—JAMES THURBER

A dog can hear sounds from up to 250 yards away.

"To his dog, every man is Napoleon; hence the constant popularity of dogs."
—ALDOUS HUXLEY

The *Odyssey*, written by Homer in the ninth century BCE, is considered one of the first writings to include mention of dogs.

"No matter how little money and how few possessions you own, having a dog makes you rich."
—Louis Sabin

On average a dog's heart beats between 70 and 120 times per minute.

"No one appreciates the very special genius of your conversation as the dog does."
—CHRISTOPHER MORLEY

The only two animals with a prostate are humans and dogs.

The first recorded use of bloodhounds as crime fighters was in 1805, when the British Thrapthon Association for the Prevention of Felons employed them to hunt down and capture poachers and thieves.

Bulldogs are so named because of the breed's past connection with bull baiting.

More than 33 percent of Americans talk to their dogs on the phone or leave messages for their pets when they are away from home.

On average, a female dog carries her young for about nine weeks before giving birth.

The hottest days of summer are known as "dog days." The association between heat and dogs stretches back at least to ancient Egypt.

In Japan, new parents are often presented with a small statue of an Akita to represent a wish of health, happiness, and long life.

The bite of a human is more likely
to cause infection than a dog's bite.

The Chihuahua is the smallest breed of dog.

"Nobody can fully understand the meaning of love unless he's owned a dog.
A dog can show you more honest affection with a flick of his tail
than a man can gather through a lifetime of handshakes."
—GENE HILL

A poodle's haircut is meant to improve his swimming abilities. The uncut hair keeps its joints warm.

"Love me, love my dog."
—Saint Bernard

Chewbacca of *Star Wars* was inspired by
George Lucas's dog Indiana, an Alaskan malamute.

More than a million canines have been named a
beneficiary in their masters' wills.

Airedales were used as messengers during times of war.

"Dogs are not our whole life, but they make our lives whole."
—Roger Caras

Some of the most popular names for female dogs are Molly, Maggie, Daisy, Lucy, Ginger, Chloe, Princess, Angel, Zoe, Sasha, Lady, Missy, Misty, and Bella.

"We give dogs time we can spare, space we can spare, and love we can spare. And in return, dogs give us their all. It's the best deal man has ever made."
—M. FACKLAM

The warmth of the sun tends to soothe and relax the muscles of old dogs.

Because of their speed, salukis were used by the Arabs
to track down gazelles, the fastest of antelopes.

"It's no coincidence that man's best friend cannot talk."
—Anonymous

The world's oldest dog lived to be 29 years and 5 months.

George Washington was the original breeder
of the American foxhound in 1770.
Washington maintained a group of more than 30 hounds.

The Irish wolfhound is the world's tallest breed.

Bernese mountain dogs were primarily herders, but may also have been used to pull carts.

"Beware of a man that does not talk and a dog that does not bark."
—PORTUGUESE PROVERB

An adult dog has 42 teeth.

The bearded collie—also known as a Beardie—is one of the oldest breeds in Britain.

The kuvasz's name comes from the corrupted spelling of the Turkish word *kawasz*, "armed guard of the nobility," and the Arabian word *kawwasz*, "archer."

"A dog believes you are what you think you are."
—JANE SWAN

The word *collie* is Scottish slang used to describe sheepdogs.

"Yesterday I was a dog. Today I'm a dog. Tomorrow I'll probably still be a dog. Sigh! There's so little hope for advancement."
—SNOOPY

Corgis were once used to drive cattle off land where they did not belong.

"A dog is not considered a good dog because he is a good barker.
A man is not considered a good man because he is a good talker."
—CHWANG TZU

Pictures of dogs resembling the Chihuahua appear in ancient paintings in Mexico.

One of the world's first space travelers
was a dog named Laika (which means "barker").
Russian scientists launched her inside a satellite in 1957.

Mixed breed dogs are less likely to suffer from inherited diseases and disabilities than purebred dogs are.

"Our dogs will love and admire the meanest of us,
and feed our colossal vanity with their uncritical homage."
—AGNES REPPLIER

The first team of Siberian huskies made its debut in the All Alaska Sweepstakes Race of 1909.

"No philosophers so thoroughly
comprehend us as dogs and horses."
—HERMAN MELVILLE

The world's tallest dog is a Great Dane from Sacramento named Gibson.
He measured seven feet when standing on its hind legs.

Due to overpopulation, more than 30,000 dogs and cats are destroyed in the United States every day.

The Irish water spaniel has a naturally water-repellent coat of hair.

"I think dogs are the most amazing creatures; they give unconditional love.
For me they are the role model for being alive."
—GILDA RADNER

A Neapolitan mastiff gave birth, via cesarean section, to the world's largest litter—24 puppies in all.

Each year, approximately five million people suffer from dog bites in the United States.

"A watchdog is a dog kept to guard your home, usually by sleeping where a burglar would awaken the household by falling over him."
—ANONYMOUS

"Outside of a dog, a book is man's best friend. Inside of a dog, it's too dark to read."
—GROUCHO MARX

A dog's normal body temperature is 100.5 to 102.5 degrees Fahrenheit.

Dogs see best in dim light.

Dogs who eat only dry food need more water
than dogs who eat wet food.

In the wild, pack dogs howl before they face danger together.
Domesticated dogs tend to howl because they are left alone.

Dogs do not have collarbones.

"Properly trained, a man can be a dog's best friend."
—Corey Ford

Before it became mandatory for dog owners in New York City to clean up after their pets, more than 40 million pounds of dog excrement littered the streets.

Sounds are amplified by the rain, which explains why many dogs would rather stay indoors when it is pouring outside.

The name *poodle* derived from the German word *puddeln*, which translates as "to splash in water."

Dogs often bark to protect their territory, both in the wild and at home.

There are an estimated 150 million dogs worldwide.

About 80 percent of dog owners buy their pets gifts for holidays and birthdays.

"The dog was created specially for children. He is the god of frolic."
—HENRY WARD BEECHER

Chewing on a bone will help to keep a dog's teeth strong and clean.

There are rent-a-dog companies in Japan that charge between 10 and 20 dollars an hour for a dog.

"If you pick up a starving dog and make him prosperous, he will not bite you; that is the principal difference between a dog and a man."
—Mark Twain

To calculate your dog's approximate age in human terms,
assume that it turns 18 years old on its first birthday.
Add 5 years to its age every year thereafter.

Approximately half of all of dog owners vacation with their pets.

"He never makes it his business to inquire whether you are in the right or wrong, never bothers as to whether you are going up or down life's ladder, never asks whether you are rich or poor, silly or wise, sinner or saint. You are his pal. That is enough for him."
—Jerome K. Jerome

"The world was conquered through the understanding of dogs;
the world exists through the understanding of dogs."
—NIETZSCHE

PHOTOGRAPHY CREDITS

The following abbreviations are used: JI—© 2007 Jupiter Images Corporation; BS—Big Stock Photo; iSP—iStockphoto.com; IO—IndexOpen; SS—ShutterStock; DV—Digital Vision; BX—Brand X Pictures; PD—PhotoDisc, Inc.; WK—Wikimedia; SB—Star Media Ltd

JI, 22, 60, 64, 84, 92, 116, 144, 184, 238, 294, 298, 310, 350, 358, 370, 392, 400, 404, 424, 442, 490, 502;BS/Michael Klenetsky, 20; BS/Tre Graves, 36; BS/Pattie Steib, 48; BS/Cindi Wilson, 88; BS/Jiri Vaclavek, 140; BS/Cris Calhoun, 182; BS/Pam McGee, 186; BS/Christine Bork, 190; BS/Geoff Delderfield, 202; BS/Sean McHaffie, 204; BS/Emmanuelle Bonzami, 264, 486; BS/Alexandr Anastasin, 268; BS/N Joy Neish, 334; BS/Monika Wisniewska, 342; BS/Steve Pepple, 408; BS/Lori Carpenter, 492; BS/Martin Smith, 494; BS/Leticia Wilson, 504; BS/Joe Gough, 510; BS/Steven Pepple, 526; BS/Patricia Marroquin, 536; iSP/Adrian Moisei, 40; iSP/Simon Mitchell, 78; iSP/Roger Branch, 94; iSP/Luis Santana, 236; iSP/ Norma Cornes, 448; iSP/Eric Isselée, 44, 452; iSP/Alexandr Anastasin, 450; iSP/Brent Miles, 460; iSP/ Nicholas Homrich, 470; iSP/Martin Pernter, 474; iSP/Tina Rencelj, 458; IO/Mistral Images, 8, 386, 524; IO/FogStock LLC , 28, 66, 80, 120, 132, 150, 174, 222, 282, 324, 326, 346, 382, 414, 508; IO/ Photos.com Select , 46, 466; IO/DesignPics Inc., 108; IO/DesignPics Inc., 154, 162, 192, 250; IO/Ralph Reinhold, 206, 216, 516; IO/Bruce Ando, 314; IO/VStock LLC, 348; SS/asian, 2, 18. 542; SS/Kevin Swop, 10; SS/Alfredo Schaufelberger, 24, 320; SS/zimmytws, 26; SS/Iztok Noc, 30; SS/Cindy Hughes, 32, 456; SS/Xorgeir Ómarsson, 34; SS/Waldemar Dabrowski, 38, 240, 276; SS/John Wollwerth, 50, 364; SS/ Naomi Hasegawa, 54; SS/Julie DeGuia, 58; SS/Michele Perbellini, 70; SS/Eric Gevaert, 72, 288; SS/Sandra Caldwell, 86; SS/Verity Johnson, 90; SS/MalibuBooks, 96; SS/Jan de Wild, 100, 246, 430, 52; SS/Steven Vona, 104; SS/Christine Nichols, 106; SS/Joy Brown, 110, 252; SS/Ingvald Kaldhussater, 112; SS/Paul Brennan, 114; SS/Dariush M., 118; SS/Wolfgang Schaller, 122; SS/Laura Stone, 128; SS/Andreas Weiss, 134; SS/ANP, 136; SS/James Klotz, 138; SS/Candice M Cunningham, 142; SS/Magdalena Szachowska,